When People Die

JOANNE E. BERNSTEIN and STEPHEN V. GULLO
photographs by ROSMARIE HAUSHERR

E. P. DUTTON   NEW YORK

The photographer thanks the Metropolitan Museum of Art for permission to photograph the burial urn (Rogers Fund, 1910) on page 26; the Fire Department of New York City for the official photo used on pages 16-17; and the many other people who helped in the making of the pictures in this book: the McCormack family; the McIver family; the Mzimela family; the Parran family; the Robles family; the Todaro family; the Wong family; Mr. Calvin Albert; Mr. Lou Boasi; Muriel Petioni, M.D.; Nursery School of the General Theological Seminary, N.Y.C.; Bellevue Hospital, N.Y.C.; Seaview Hospital, Staten Island, N.Y.; the Children of 15th Street, N.Y.C.; Gutterman's Inc. (Funeral Directors) ; Visit America, Inc.

Library of Congress Cataloging in Publication Data

Bernstein, Joanne E.   When people die

SUMMARY: Explains in simple terms the reasons for death, theories on afterlife, burial practices, grief, and the naturalness of death in the chain of life.

1. Death—Juvenile literature.   [1. Death]
I. Gullo, Stephen V., joint author.   II. Hausherr, Rosmarie.   III. Title.
BD444.B46   128'.5   76-23099   ISBN 0-525-42545-4

Published simultaneously in Canada by Clarke, Irwin & Company Limited, Toronto and Vancouver

Editor: Ann Troy   Designer: Riki Levinson

Printed in the U.S.A.   First Edition   10 9 8 7 6 5 4 3 2 1

For Robin and Andrew
J.E.B.

For Rose, Maurene, Christian, Matthew,
Drs. Fleischer, Kutscher, and D. Yakir
S.V.G.

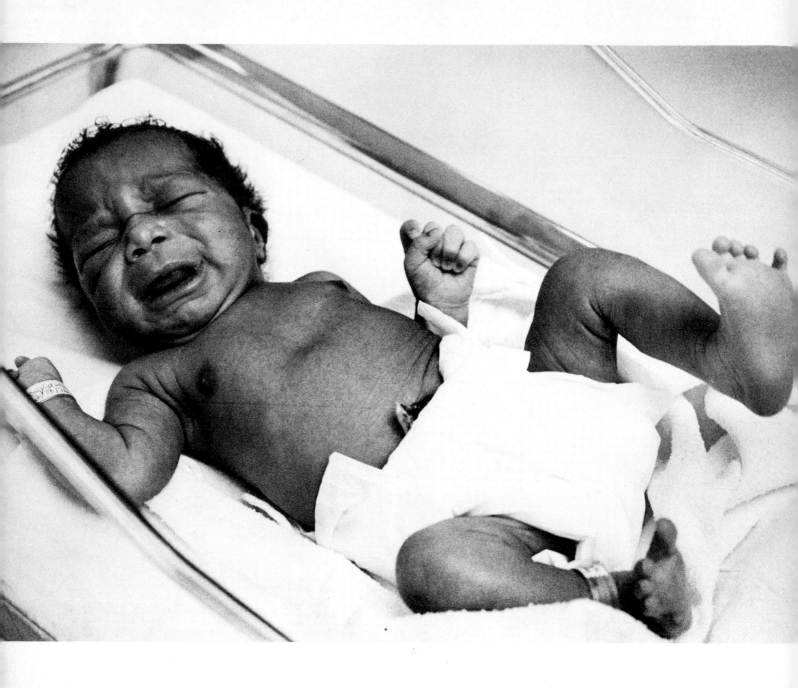

For everything there is a time. There is a time to be born, a time to live, and a time to die.

Mrs. Michaelson died last week. She was eighty-two years old. She shared her life with her two children, three grand-children, and one great grandchild.

Mrs. Michaelson was the principal of the Harris Park Elementary School. She also taught first grade for many years. She loved the moment when children began to read by themselves, and children loved her.

When Mrs. Michaelson finished working and retired, she
occupied herself by reading, taking long walks, and playing
the guitar. She started to write books for young children.

She enjoyed reading them to boys and girls in her neighborhood. Whenever she had time, she visited her family. She was particularly happy when she played with her great grandson David.

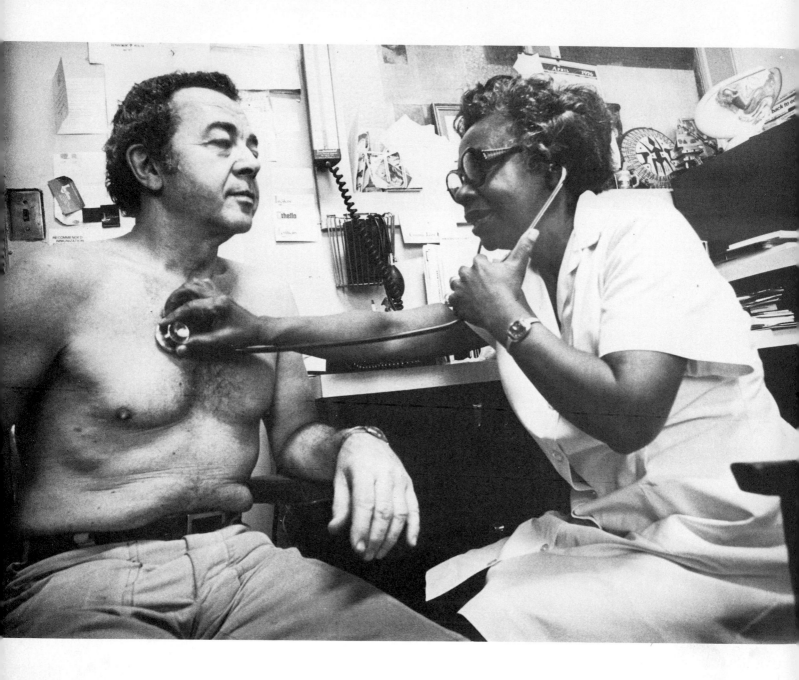

People die because they have lived. Death is a part of everyone's life. All human beings die because, while they have been living, their bodies have been gradually wearing down.

The parts of the body break down ever so slowly, in an aging process which begins at birth. Children's bodies do a great deal of growing and very little breaking down. Adults' bodies do very little growing and start to break down more rapidly. By the end of the aging process, the body can no longer keep itself going. This is normally the time when people die.

Most people live for many, many years. Most people live until they have had a chance to accomplish some of the things which are important to them.

For all men and women, loving people and being loved is important.

For many men and women, seeing their children and grandchildren grow up is important.

For many men and women, working at jobs
they enjoy is important.

People try to stay in good health. They try to live for many, many years, as Mrs. Michaelson did.

But some people do not have the chance to live until they are very old. People occasionally become so seriously ill that vital parts of their bodies break down, and they die.

People occasionally die in disasters. Some die in floods and fires. Others die in accidents, especially automobile crashes.

Most of the time, human beings try to avoid hurting each other and themselves. There are troubled times, though, when people deliberately kill one another or even themselves. This is what happens in murder, suicide, and war.

Doctors and scientists tell us that death does not hurt.

When people die, the parts of their bodies stop functioning. Their hearts stop beating. Their brains stop working.

They do not hear, feel, speak, or think. They are no longer aware of the world around them.

Before doctors say that a person is dead, they are very careful to check for all signs of life.

They check to see if the heart is beating. They check to see if the person's eyes react to light. If the eyes blink, doctors know that the brain is working.

If there is still any doubt, the doctors might use an electro-encephalograph to see if the brain is working. This machine measures brain waves.

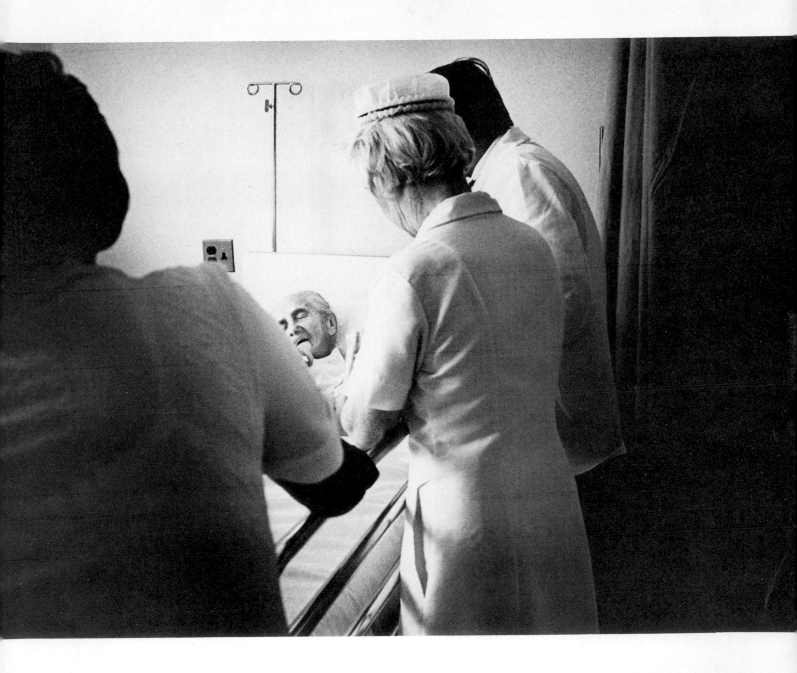

We do not know everything about dying. While scientists know what happens to the body, there are many different beliefs about what happens to the spirit.

The spirit is everything about a person except the body. Sometimes the spirit is called the soul. The soul is the thoughts, wishes, and feelings of the person. It is all those qualities which make one person different from all the others in the world.

People have always wondered what becomes of the spirit after death.

Over the years, in various parts of the world, the question has been answered differently.

Today, religious Christians believe that the soul lives on happily in heaven. There it will dwell in the presence of God. Moslems have a similar idea about life after death for the soul.

Some religious Jews share this belief. Others are not certain and do not emphasize life after death.

In many Eastern religions, such as Hinduism, there is also

a belief in an afterlife for the soul. They see life and death as part of a circle which includes dying and being born again on earth. The soul will continue its life in a new person or other living creature. This idea is called reincarnation, and it is even held by some people who do not have any religion.

In addition, there have always been people of many backgrounds who do not think the soul exists at all.

After a person dies, the person's family often plans a funeral. The funeral is a way of saying a final good-bye. The person is dead and will never be seen on earth again.

This is what happened in Mrs. Michaelson's family. All of Mrs. Michaelson's friends and relatives came together in one place. Her children and grandchildren were there. The teachers from Harris Park Elementary School were there. Her neighbors were there, and so were the students she had known over the years.

They talked about why they liked Mrs. Michaelson and how sad they were to say good-bye.

In our country, after people die, in most cases their bodies are buried or cremated. In burial, the body is put into a box called a casket. It is placed in the earth. Special pieces of land set aside for this purpose are known as cemeteries.

In cremation, heat is used to reduce the body to ashes. The ashes may be scattered over the earth or into the sea, in a place which the person had enjoyed while alive. Or they may be put in an urn for burial in a cemetery.

In other countries, customs may be different. Often in Spain, caskets are not placed in the earth but above ground in vertical rows.

In parts of India, bodies are sometimes placed in a ravine and covered with stones.

In Nigeria, many people prefer to be buried on their own land, next to their relatives who have died.

In time, bodies and scattered ashes become part of the earth. This process is called decomposition.

Decomposition nourishes the soil. It helps to feed the plants, animals, and people which live off the earth. In this way, those who are dead still contribute to the life cycle of the universe.

You may feel many different ways when a person you love dies.

You may find it hard to believe that the person is dead.

You may not want to eat. You may be very tired and unable to sleep. Your body may ache all over, and you may feel empty inside.

You may feel sad and lonely. You may not want to ride a bike or visit friends. You may be angry toward the person who died and left you.

Or you may not feel any of these things, but may have different feelings instead. The changes in you are called grief.

Most of us grieve when someone we love dies. It is normal and healthy.

Gradually, as time goes on, we feel better and return to our usual ways.

We slowly begin to realize that the person will never return.

We begin to eat and sleep as we always have. The aches in our bodies fade. We feel less empty.

We want to see our friends. We start to enjoy doing things with them.

In time, we will begin to laugh again.

It is good to ask any questions you have about what is happening to you. It is good to talk about how you feel. That usually makes the hurt go away faster.

This is what Mrs. Michaelson's children and grandchildren did. They shared their sadness. They also remembered the times they had with her and realized how much she had given them.

They realized that in some ways they were very much like Mrs. Michaelson. They loved books and music, just as she did. They laughed at the same jokes. Some of them even had noses similar to hers.

The things that they remember about her will always remain part of their lives.

Each of us is a part of a great chain of life. For everything there is a time: there is a time to be born, a time to live, and a time to die.

Joanne E. Bernstein is Assistant Professor of Early Childhood Education at Brooklyn College. She specializes in children's literature and also reviews children's books. She and her husband have two children and live in Brooklyn.

Stephen V. Gullo is a psychologist and Assistant Professor, School of Education, Brooklyn College. He has served as Co-Director of the Family Bereavement Project, College of Physicians and Surgeons, Columbia University. Dr. Gullo is a member of the Professional Advisory Board of the Foundation of Thanatology in New York.

Rosmarie Hausherr is a freelance photographer. She received her training in her native Switzerland, and her photographs have appeared in European magazines and newspapers. Ms. Hausherr now lives in New York. This is the first book she has illustrated with her photographs.